A brief guide

Weymouth, Portland and Dorchester

(and surrounding area)

text and photographs by Robert Westwood

Inspiring Places Publishing
2 Down Lodge Close
Alderholt
Fordingbridge
SP63JA

ISBN 978-0-9564104-2-9

Contents

Photo: Osmington Mills

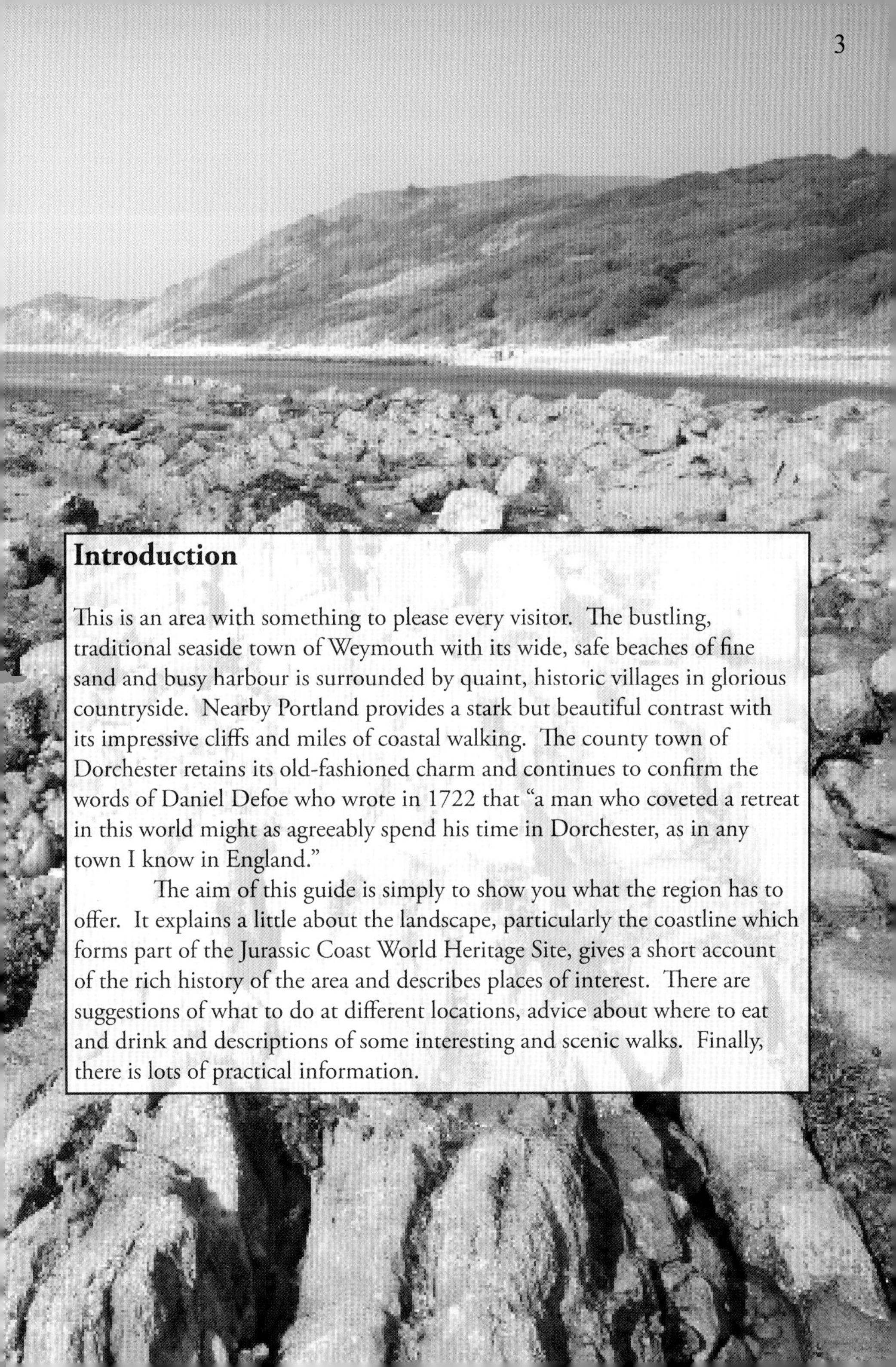

Introduction

This is an area with something to please every visitor. The bustling, traditional seaside town of Weymouth with its wide, safe beaches of fine sand and busy harbour is surrounded by quaint, historic villages in glorious countryside. Nearby Portland provides a stark but beautiful contrast with its impressive cliffs and miles of coastal walking. The county town of Dorchester retains its old-fashioned charm and continues to confirm the words of Daniel Defoe who wrote in 1722 that "a man who coveted a retreat in this world might as agreeably spend his time in Dorchester, as in any town I know in England."

The aim of this guide is simply to show you what the region has to offer. It explains a little about the landscape, particularly the coastline which forms part of the Jurassic Coast World Heritage Site, gives a short account of the rich history of the area and describes places of interest. There are suggestions of what to do at different locations, advice about where to eat and drink and descriptions of some interesting and scenic walks. Finally, there is lots of practical information.

Landscape and Geology

Gentle rolling hills, wooded valleys, sparkling rivers and streams, quaint villages built of local stone and a dramatic and varied coastline; this area has much to please and interest the visitor. Circling around it are rich Chalk downlands with picturesque villages nestled in quiet valleys. Below the Chalk are gently dipping layers of Jurassic sediments, stretching to the sea; limestones, silts and clays that form rich farmland. As we travel from Dorchester to Weymouth the Chalk ends abruptly at a ridge that runs west to east and seems to form a natural boundary to the Weymouth/Portland area and its hinterland. In the warmer climate of the Bronze Age the Chalk downlands were densely populated and burial remains from this ancient civilisation are scattered all over the present landscape. Huge fields are characteristic of the Chalk uplands, making a stark contrast with the patchwork of smaller fields lower down, something that Thomas Hardy famously described in *Tess of the D'Urbervilles* as the eponymous heroine looked down on the Vale of Blackmore.

All of the rocks of the area are sediments laid down in ancient seas. The Chalk is made almost entirely of organic remains of microscopic

Below: This is a simplified map of the geology of Dorset. The area covered by the guide is shown by the square at the bottom. In the key the oldest rocks (Jurassic) are shown at the bottom, the youngest at the top. (Steinsky, 2007)

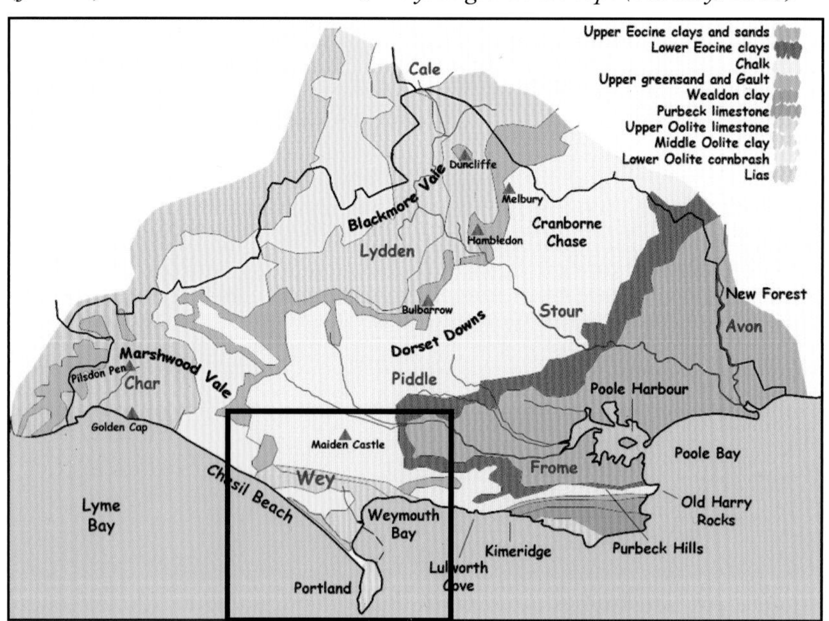

algae known as coccolithophores and foraminifera. The absence of material eroded from land suggests that waterless deserts may have surrounded the shallow, tropical Chalk sea. The Jurassic sediments are again marine in origin, deposited in seas of varying depth. The richly coloured limestones are also partly organic in origin, the calcium carbonate coming from the myriad creatures with shells that existed in the Jurassic oceans, but often mixed with much eroded detritus and sometimes suggesting formation in a high energy environment, i.e. a shallow sea with much wave action.

The Jurassic Coast

The coastline of the region forms part of the Jurassic Coast World Heritage Site that stretches from Exmouth in East Devon to Studland Bay. The rocks along the coast were formed in three geological periods, the Triassic, Jurassic and Cretaceous and range from 250 million years old at the beginning of the Triassic to a mere 65 million years old at the end of the Cretaceous. The coast between Abbotsbury and Ringstead is composed of Jurassic sediments, although Chesil Beach is a much more recent structure. The whole era comprising the three periods is significant because at the beginning and end of it were major extinctions when most of life on the planet died out, the latter one, when the dinosaurs were amongst the casualties, is now generally agreed to have been caused by the impact of a giant meteorite. In between these two cataclysmic events life recovered and evolved afresh, developing into a world we sometimes perceive as dominated by dinosaurs. In truth, many weird and wonderful creatures graced the planet during this time and it is the fossils they left that have made the Jurassic Coast such an important resource for our understanding of the evolution of life on Earth.

Why is it that this 85 mile stretch of coastline contains such a collection of fossils? Firstly it is because of the area's geographical location throughout the 185 million years of this "Mesozoic" era. At the start of the era all of the Earth's landmass was concentrated in one huge supercontinent geologists have named Pangaea. As this started to break up what we now call Devon and Dorset were near one of the lines of splitting and were under a shallow sea, but still near to land. This basic picture continued throughout the era and the sedimentary rocks of the Jurassic Coast were formed in a variety of environments with land never very far away; often ideally situated for the preservation as fossils of many forms of life. Secondly, these rocks now form a coastline, much of which is rapidly eroding and so continually revealing its precious record of life in the Mesozoic.

I will deal with Chesil Beach and The Fleet separately as they are unique and very recent features geologically speaking, so our look at the Jurassic Coast of the area will begin with the Isle of Portland. Not quite an island, being joined to the mainland by a narrow isthmus at the end of Chesil Beach, Portland nevertheless has the feel of an island, giving the visitor the idea that he or she has entered somewhere different. Famous for its quarries of what is reputedly the best building stone in the world, Portland has long been a place of hard, manual labour that has nurtured a tough, fiercely independent population.

Portland Stone is known as an "oolitic" limestone and formed in a shallow, tropical sea towards the end of the Jurassic period around 100 million years ago. Look at it closely and you may notice it is formed of millions of tiny spherical balls or ooliths. These are made from calcium carbonate precipitated from the dissolved hard parts of shell creatures. It gathered around tiny sand particles or shell fragments as they were rolled backwards and forwards by wave action at the bottom of a shallow sea. Similar conditions exist today off the coast of the Bahamas. The limestones contain many fossils of shell creatures like ammonites and oysters. Layers of the Portland Stone lie sloping gently southwards, facilitating the splitting

Below: Old quarry workings at Portland Bill.

and removal of blocks for dressing and transportation.

Stone was being quarried at Portland in Roman times, as evidenced by its use in buildings of the period. By the 14th century it was being widely exported and its use continued to grow. After a period of decline further expansion began in the 17th century, especially after the Great Fire, when Christopher Wren chose Portland Stone for much of the rebuilding of London, including his new design for St. Paul's Cathedral. The census of 1851 reveals that over one fifth of the male population of Portland was directly involved in the quarrying. Today the quarries are largely deserted but some stone is still produced and used for a variety of purposes.

Above: A small waterfall on the beach at Osmington Mills.

Above the Portland Stone lie the Purbeck strata, recognisable as much thinner layers. These are limestones formed in shallow, freshwater lagoons through which dinosaurs waded.

East of Weymouth the cliffs are composed of older Jurassic sediments, grits, clays, sands and limestones formed, again, in a shallow tropical sea. At Osmington Mills the rocks are about 155 million years old and the limestones are well exposed, lying in layers dipping almost vertically and running parallel to the coast. Naturally they were deposited as horizontal layers on the sea bed and have been tilted by great earth movements.

Two of the walks detailed later will allow you to see and appreciate features of the Jurassic Coast.

Chesil Beach and the Fleet

Geologically speaking, Chesil beach is a very recent phenomenon, reaching its present state only about 4-5000 years ago. It is a world famous example of a storm beach and has been created by wave action driving material eastwards along the coast; much of the energy coming from storms that, while infrequent from our perspective, are relatively frequent on a geological timescale. It is generally accepted that much of the material was deposited on the floor of Lyme Bay by fast, south flowing rivers as glacial ice melted around 15000 years ago. It is important to remember that Lyme Bay was above sea level then, but, as more glacial ice melted, the sea level rose and the sand and gravel that had been dumped was carried eastwards by the waves, building the first version of Chesil Beach. Then about 5000 years ago, as the sea level rose further, previously land locked older cliffs were eroded and the detritus again carried eastwards, completing the formation of Chesil Beach, an older sandy core being overlain by shingle.

The Fleet lagoon was created by the beach being pushed northwards and this process is continuing; the beach is edging inland by about 15cm per year. The Fleet is brackish water with fresh water entering via streams and springs on the landward side and seawater seeping through Chesil Beach. Most of the Fleet is no more than 2 metres deep.

Many shipwrecks have been recorded off Chesil Beach with fierce south-westerly winds driving vessels on to the shingle. In 1824 a storm struck that devastated the village of East Fleet and much of the surrounding area. Ships were carried over the beach into the Fleet and it is said that, at the old church, the water was 30 feet deep!

Main picture: The Fleet at Rodden Hive near Langton Herring. *(see walk page 34)*

Inset: Chesil Beach, just west of Abbotsbury.

History

There is much of historical interest in this area. To begin with there is evidence of ancient civilisations on almost every hillside; Bronze Age (roughly 2000 – 800 BC) people have left their mark all over Dorset in the shape of round barrows in which they buried their dead. As well as sometimes containing gold items, the barrows often held clay beakers, leading to the name "Beaker People". Bronkham Hill, south-west of Dorchester, has many of these round barrows. The Iron Age people who followed left their own distinctive monuments in the shape of hillforts which again are widespread in Dorset. Perhaps the most famous example is Maiden Castle near Dorchester, the scene of bitter fighting against the Romans in AD 43. Dorchester subsequently became the administrative centre of the region in Roman times, covering an area of around 70-80 acres. Parts of the Roman town wall can still be seen as can the remains of an amphitheatre at Maumbury Rings. Weymouth, too, was a Roman settlement and boasts the remains of a Roman temple overlooking the bay on Jordan Hill. Roman villas have been excavated at Preston and on the Isle of Portland. Portland Stone was used by the Romans in the building of Dorchester, so the history of quarrying there goes back to at least these times.

In the year 787 the Anglo-Saxon Chronicle records that the first Viking raid took place in Portland, the precursor to many that were to shake the peaceful and prosperous civilisation that had developed there since Roman times. Portland was also the scene of a battle with the Danish army in 837. Interestingly, the first recorded use of the word "Dorset" comes from the Anglo-Saxon Chronicle, deriving from the Old English "Dornsaete" and simply meaning people who lived around Dorchester.

1348 was a dark year in English history, for that was when a merchant ship docked at Weymouth and brought the Black Death to these shores; the town and surrounding countryside were quick to suffer. In the English Civil War there were battles at Abbotsbury and Weymouth, where there was bloody fighting on the streets for several days.

There are many interesting places to visit where this rich history can be appreciated. Opposite is a list of the main ones; some are described in more detail elsewhere, in which case a page reference is given.

Historic Sites of the Area

Dorchester - museums, Thomas Hardy sites, Maumbury Rings. (page 17)
Abbotsbury - swannery, St. Catherine's Chapel, tithe barn. (page 20)
Hardy's Monument – SY613877. Monument to the other Hardy, Admiral Sir Thomas Hardy, captain of HMS Victory at Trafalgar. This is a good place to start a walk along **Bronkham Hill**, site of many Bronze Age round barrows. (page 25)
Nine Stones, Winterbourne Abbas – SY610904. A Neolithic stone circle beside the A35.
Maiden Castle – SY665885 (page 24)
Weymouth - old harbour, Nothe Fort, (page 12)
Jordan Hill Roman Temple – SY700822. The foundations of a Roman temple, probably used in the 4th century.
Athelhampton – SY770942. A beautiful Elizabethan manor house and gardens. (page 26)
Cerne Abbas - Giant, abbey remains, Silver Well. (page 22)
Portland - old quarries, Portland Bill, Portland Castle. (page 15)

Old Weymouth Harbour

Weymouth

There has been a settlement at Weymouth for hundreds of years; the ports at Weymouth and Melcombe Regis were being written about as early as the 11th century. There were originally two towns with Melcombe being to the east of the river and Weymouth to the west. Melcombe Regis was to gain notoriety in 1348 when a merchant ship from Venice docking there introduced the Black Death to England. The two towns and the hinterland were quickly devastated.

For several hundred years the towns were oriented towards the river and the harbour, the sea front was not developed. By the late 18th century Weymouth's importance as a port was declining, its harbour with narrow quays was not suitable for larger ships plying foreign trade and it engaged mostly in coastal trade. In 1781 Weymouth had no ships registered for foreign trade. Fortunately for the town its prosperity was saved by becoming a centre for privateers. Privateers were legalised pirates given a commission by the King to attack and plunder ships from countries Britain was at war with. It was a profitable business; in 1775 there were 65 seamen in Weymouth, by 1810 there were 2188!

Predating slightly the rise of Weymouth as a centre for privateers was its development as a resort. Sea bathing began to be popular in the mid 18th century and Weymouth (now unified as one town) soon began to attract wealthy and powerful patrons, culminating in 1789 with the arrival of the convalescing King George III. He visited regularly between 1791 and 1802 and Weymouth's popularity grew accordingly. The illicit smuggling industry also did rather well at this time; thousands of the king's followers created a ready market for contraband. Throughout Victorian times Weymouth continued to attract wealthy and famous visitors and the esplanade became lined with imposing houses. It has remained a popular resort ever since.

Things to do:

- Swim and have fun on the beach – Weymouth has some of the finest sand in Britain.
- Visit one of the many tourist attractions: Sea Life Park, Sharky's, Weymouth Timewalk, Discovery Centre, Weymouth Museum, Deep Sea Adventure, Cineworld.
- Visit Lodmoor Country Park and Radipole Lake Nature Reserve.
- Visit Bennett's Water Gardens.
- Go shopping at Brewer's Quay.
- Visit Nothe Fort.

Some of Weymouth's Attractions

The Nothe Fort

Work on Nothe Fort began in 1860 and it was finally commissioned in 1872. Around this time coastal defence establishments had been constructed all along the south coast to guard important military installations, notably the ring of forts protecting the Navy's largest base at Portsmouth. These defences, known as Palmerston Forts after the Prime Minister at the time, had been built following a Royal Commission to investigate the threat of a French invasion.

Built on three levels with the middle level home to long range muzzle loaded cannons, Nothe Fort was updated with new artillery during World War I and again during World War II when it served as an important anti-aircraft defence. Although its guns were only fired in anger during the Second World War, the fort has been important protection for Royal Navy ships anchored in Portland Harbour. It continued in active use until 1956 when it was sold by the Navy to the local council. After many years of neglect it has now been transformed into an interesting museum, which, with its spectacular location, makes for a great day out.

Below: the Nothe Fort.

Bennett's Water Gardens

Built on the site of old brick pits, Bennett's Water Gardens (above) are eight acres of ornamental ponds and wooded glades; an ideal place to relax and unwind. Here is one of the country's finest collections of water lilies with around 150 species blooming from spring through to autumn. There is also a stylish restaurant, the Café Monet, to finish your tour. The gardens are open from mid-March to the end of October.

The Old Harbour and Brewer's Quay

Brewer's Quay is a complex of shops, cafés and inns on the site of an old Victorian brewery by the old harbour. It is also the home to several interesting tourist attractions, namely the Discovery Centre, Weymouth Museum and Timewalk.

The old harbour occupies the mouth of the River Wey and is a perfect place to wander round and sit outside at one of the many cafés, pubs and restaurants. Originally Weymouth was on the south side of the harbour and Melcombe Regis on the north side. There was often friction between the two towns over the use of the harbour, a problem solved by Elizabeth I who declared that they should both be part of one borough.

The Isle of Portland

The Isle of Portland has a distinct character, very different in feeling from its sprawling tourist oriented neighbour Weymouth. The great collector of Dorset folklore J S Udal, writing in 1922, says that the inhabitants of Portland, "say that they are Phoenicians, have never, until lately, allowed any English, or 'foreigners', as they term us, to hold land in their territory, but have kept themselves a distinct people". Thomas Hardy called Portland "the Isle of Slingers", a reference to the fact that Iron Age peoples used pebbles from Chesil Beach as ammunition for their slings.

Today the people of Portland are more welcoming! There is now much for the tourist, although perhaps of a different nature to Weymouth. To understand its character and its history a note about the geology is important. The surface rocks of Portland are predominantly the Portland and Purbeck limestones, sloping gently southwards. It is this structure that has allowed the Portland Stone to be quarried and transported to the sea for export. It has also been responsible for a spectacular coastline to explore and walk along.

Portland Stone was being quarried in Roman times and was used for important buildings, for example in Dorchester. By the 14th century the stone was being exported for major building projects such as Exeter Cathedral and buildings in London. The industry thrived in the 17th century when Portland Stone was used extensively in the rebuilding of London after the Great Fire. In the 19th and early 20th centuries Portland Stone quarries were still flourishing; in 1914 over 100 000 tons of the stone were exported. Although the scale of the industry has declined, it continues to thrive and the beautiful limestone is still in demand.

One of the major quarries, Tout, has been transformed into a sculpture park and its setting on the north-western edge of the island with magnificent views along the coast makes it well worth a visit.

Things to do:

- Visit Portland Castle, owned by English Heritage.
- Enjoy a walk along the coast. (see page 34)
- Visit Tout Quarry Sculpture Park.
- Visit Portland Museum at Church Ope Cove.
- Visit Portland Bill and the lighthouse and visitor centre.
- Relax on the beach and have a swim at Church Ope Cove.
- Visit the Chesil Beach Centre.
- Book a course at the Portland and Weymouth National Sailing Academy.

Portland's beautiful coastline has many reminders of its quarrying heritage. The main picture shows the east coast of Portland with sheer cliffs of massively bedded Portland Stone, ideal building stone. Inset is Tout Quarry Sculpture Park in the north-west corner of the isle. The first workings were on the southern tip of Portland where it was possible for the split stone to be gently slid forward into boats.

Dorchester

Dorchester is an attractive and thriving county town. There has been a settlement here since before Roman times. Maumbury Rings, on the edge of the modern town, is a Neolithic henge monument later transformed by the Romans into an amphitheatre. It was begun around 2500 BC. In the Iron Age a settlement was situated on the nearby hill of Maiden Castle, one of the most impressive of Dorset's many Iron Age hillforts. Excavations have revealed a bloody battle between the Romans and the local Durotriges in AD43; some fascinating artefacts are on display in Dorset County Museum. Following this conquest the Roman town was developed on the present site and Dorchester has been a market centre for the region ever since. The present town contains many Georgian buildings, partly a result of serious fires in the 17th and 18th centuries.

A number of historical events are associated with Dorchester. In the English Civil War the town was held by Parliament and heavily defended against Royalist forces, while in 1685 the town was the setting for the "Bloody Assizes" where the infamous Judge Jeffries meted out harsh punishments to those who had supported the ill-fated rebellion led by James, Duke of Monmouth. In 1834 Dorchester held another landmark trial, that of the Tolpuddle Martyrs (see page 27).

Dorchester, of course, is known the world over as the home of Thomas Hardy. He was born in nearby Bockhampton and lived for many years at Max Gate in Dorchester. His heart is buried in the churchyard at Stinsford, near the cottage where he was born and grew up. The Dorset County Museum has a special section on Thomas Hardy, including a replica of his study at Max Gate.

Things to do:

- Do one of the town walks. (details from TIC and see page 31)
- Visit the Dorset County Museum.
- Visit Maiden Castle. (see page 24)
- Visit the other museums – Dinosaur, Tutankhamun, Terracotta Warriors, Teddy Bear and Keep Military Museum.
- Enjoy the shops, pubs and restaurants.
- Visit the Roman Town House in the grounds of County Hall. Entrance is free and it is open all year.
- Visit Maumbury Rings Roman amphitheatre.
- Visit the Thomas Hardy sites. (see following section)
- Visit Wolfeton House, a beautiful medieval and Elizabethan house at Charminster, just north of Dorchester.

Thomas Hardy sites in and around Dorchester:

Below: The cottage at Higher Bockhampton where Hardy was born and grew up. It was here that he wrote "Far from the Madding Crowd".

The cottage is owned by the National Trust and is open to the public (near Stinsford, off A35 east of Dorchester).

Left: Dorchester high street just below the museum which has a replica of Hardy's study at Max Gate.

The Kings Arms Hotel features in "The Mayor of Casterbridge" and "Far from the Madding Crowd".

Left: The church at Stinsford which Hardy attended as a boy and where his father played violin in the choir.

Right: Hardy's heart is buried in this grave in the churchyard at Stinsford, along with his first wife Emma.

Below: Athelhampton House, visited a number of times by Hardy and immortalised in his poem "The Dame of Athelhall". Hardy's father worked on the house as a stonemason. (Athelhampton is near Puddletown, about 4 miles east of Dorchester.)

Stinsford churchyard is near Kingston Maurward. (SY 712910)

Max Gate is owned by the National Trust and is open to the public. From 2011 a new tenant has opened up most of the house for viewing. Check opening times.

Right: Max Gate in Dorchester, the house Hardy designed himself and where he lived from 1885. (near junction of A35 and A352)

Background picture is the Blackmore Vale from Bulbarrow, a favourite spot of Hardy's and remembered in the poem "Wessex Heights".

Abbotsbury

Abbotsbury is situated at the western end of the Fleet lagoon. It is a delightful village built out of the local honey coloured Jurassic limestone with many cottages dating from the 16th and 17th centuries. The reeds that grow in the brackish waters of the Fleet provide an ideal nesting environment for birds, and the monks in the Benedictine monastery, that had been founded in the 11th century by King Canute, used it to farm swans for fresh meat. This practice continued until the dissolution of the monastery in 1539; today it is the only managed nesting colony of mute swans anywhere in the world.

In 1644 the manor at Abbotsbury was owned by the Strangways family, staunch Royalists. Sir James Strangways commanded the Royalist garrison which was besieged by the forces of Parliament. Some bitter fighting ensued before the Parliamentarians were victorious and the pulpit of the local church of St. Nicholas still shows bullet holes from the encounter.

Part of the old abbey is now looked after by English Heritage and is open to all, while a tithe barn, completed in the late 14th century, now forms part of a children's farm, run by Abbotsbury Tourism who also run the Swannery and the Sub-tropical Gardens.

Below: the village of Abbotsbury.

Situated on a hill overlooking Abbotsbury is St. Catherine's Chapel, built in the first half of the 15th century, probably as a place of pilgrimage attached to the abbey. It is associated with a local "wishing" custom; as the patron saint of spinsters it is said that women used to visit St. Catherine's Chapel seeking for help to obtain a husband.

Things to do:

- Visit the Swannery, Sub-tropical Gardens and the Children's Farm.
- Have a look at Chesil Beach. (car park just down the road from the Sub-tropical Gardens)
- Walk up to St. Catherine's Chapel and admire one of the best views of Chesil Beach and the Fleet.
- Enjoy the quaint village and have something to eat and drink in one of the pubs, tea rooms or restaurants.
- Go for a scenic walk. (see page 36)

Cerne Abbas

Nestling snugly at the foot of Chalk downlands, Cerne Abbas is one of the most picturesque and atmospheric of Dorset villages. It is, of course, famous as the location of the Giant, a 180 feet long figure cut in the chalk hillside. Experts still cannot say for sure when it was made, the earliest reference to it is in the 17th century, but its style and proximity to an Iron Age earthwork suggest an ancient origin. Naturally legends have grown up around it, mostly concerning cures for infertility. During the 19th century it was fenced off to discourage practices associated with these legends! Today it is still fenced off, but the motive is conservation; however, if you do want to walk on the giant, be on top of the hill at dawn on May 1st. Every year members of the Wessex Morris Men dance in the small earthwork on top of Giant Hill and spectators are welcomed.

Cerne Abbas has much more to offer than the Giant and it is well worth exploring one of Dorset's most delightful and little known corners. The village once had a prosperous Benedictine monastery and its remains, although meagre, are both charming and evocative. At the corner of the churchyard is the Silver Well, thought to be the site where a Saxon prince, Edwold, disillusioned with war, set up a hermitage to spend the rest of his days. He had been pursuing a vision of a silver well and found it here at Cerne; he was later canonised. The well is also associated with Saint Augustine, although this may be an invention of scheming monks to attract more pilgrims. He is said to have converted the people here and struck the ground with his staff, whereby a spring gushed forth. It must be one of the few such places where what actually happened is probably more fascinating and appealing than the legend!

Things to do:

- See the giant.
- Visit the Silver Well.
- Go for a walk. (see page 29)
- See the remains of the monastery.
- Have something to eat or drink in one of the pubs or tea rooms.

Opposite main picture: The Abbot's Hospice, Cerne Abbas, part of the old Benedictine monastery.
Inset top right: The Silver Well.
Inset bottom left: The face of the giant at dawn on May Day. The village is in the background.

Maiden Castle

Lying just south of Dorchester, Maiden Castle is the largest and perhaps the most impressive Iron Age hillfort in Europe; its ramparts are visible for miles around. It was here in, AD 43, that a Roman legion, under the command of the future emperor Vespasian, prepared for what to them must have been a routine operation. Around 200 families and their warriors from the Durotriges tribe lived on the hill and it boasted stout defences. Piles of pebbles from Chesil Beach had been collected and stored as ammunition for the expert slingers. It was to no avail, the Romans quickly took the fort and it was never used again for defensive purposes. Excavations have revealed a bloody battle took place with a great many bodies piled up near one of the main gates to the hillfort. There is a very informative display in the Dorset County Museum in Dorchester, including a piece of backbone of one of the defenders, still with the bolt from a Roman crossbow buried in it.

Today Maiden Castle is easily accessed from Dorchester and is well signposted from the ring road to the south of the town. Visitors can explore the whole site and the views from the ramparts are impressive.

Hardy's Monument and Bronkham Hill

Above: Hardy's Monument from Bronkham Hill, note barrow in foreground.

Near the picturesque village of Portesham is Hardy's Monument, a 72 feet high tower built to commemorate the life of Vice Admiral Sir Thomas Hardy, commander of HMS Victory and Nelson's Flag Captain at the Battle of Trafalgar. Hardy lived in Portesham during his childhood. The monument stands high on the Chalk ridge and commands stunning views over the countryside and coast.

Just to the south-east of Hardy's Monument is Bronkham Hill. This is a continuation of the Chalk ridge and the Dorset Ridgeway follows the top of it. It is covered by many Bronze Age round barrows and must have been a site of great significance at that time. The Bronze Age spans a huge period of time from around 2000 BC to 700-800 BC. During this time the inhabitants continued to bury their dead [or at least some of them] in stone chambers covered with earth. Once it was discovered, in the 19th century, that many contained interesting artefacts and that some, presumably the resting place of local leaders, contained gold items, the barrows were excavated and their contents looted. Fortunately for posterity many were excavated systematically by General Pitt-Rivers, the great Dorset philanthropist generally regarded as the father of modern archaeology.

There is parking space at the Hardy Monument and it is a great place for a picnic, a short stroll or a longer walk.

Puddletown, Athelhampton and Tolpuddle

Athelhampton is a beautiful manor house built in about 1485 by Sir William Martyn who was to become the Lord Mayor of London in 1492. It is on the site of a much earlier manor, the Saxon name suggests it was the farm ["ham"] or enclosure ["ton"] of "Athel" or "Aethel". Soon after the Conquest the manor passed into Norman hands. The house has been added to over the centuries and has remained in private hands for over 500 years. It is reputedly one of the most haunted houses in England with, unusually, its most famous ghost being that of an ape, a family pet of the Martyn family in the 16th century. After the death of the last lord of the manor the creature was apparently trapped in a secret staircase and starved to death. Other ghosts include phantom duellists dating from the Civil War.

Athelhampton and its beautiful gardens are open to the public every day except Friday and Saturday March to October and Sundays only November to February. It is on the A35 just east of Puddletown

In nearby **Puddletown** is the wonderful parish church, some of it dating back to Norman times. Inside is the tomb of Sir William Martyn, with a superb carved effigy of him. At his feet lies not a dog, as was common for such carvings, but a grinning monkey [see right], the symbol of the Martyn family. Puddletown is Weatherbury in Thomas Hardy's novels and the church was the scene of the marriage of Bathsheba and Gabriel Oak in *Far from the Madding Crowd.*

If you carry on the road past Athelhampton you will soon arrive in **Tolpuddle**, famous as the birthplace of the Trade Union movement and home of the Tolpuddle Martyrs who were deported in 1834 for swearing an illegal oath. You can visit an excellent museum housed in what were originally memorial cottages built in 1934. In the village centre is the Martyrs' tree, over 300 years old and the meeting place for the Martyrs as they discussed how to save their families from starvation.

Osmington Mills and Ringstead

There is not much besides a pub, a few houses and a holiday park at Osmington Mills, but it is a lovely little bay where the richly coloured Jurassic limestone outcrops on the shoreline. It is possible to do an easy walk to neighbouring Ringstead Bay (page 30) and return for something to eat and drink in the Smugglers' Inn. As the name suggests, Osmington was a centre for the illicit trade in the 18th and early 19th centuries and the pub was the headquarters of a notorious smuggler called "French Peter" who landed contraband brandy in the bay. The pub dates from the 13th century and was previously called the Crown. Its present name, only adopted in 1970, was formerly a nickname.

Ringstead Bay has a long pebbly beach although some sand is exposed at low tide. It is quiet and unspoilt with a car park and small shop and café just behind the beach. It too was used by smugglers and today is popular with fossil hunters.

Things to do:

- Have a meal/drink in the Smugglers' Inn.
- Explore the rock pools and ledges at Osmington.
- Have a swim at Ringstead.
- Walk from Osmington to Ringstead and back, or vice versa. (see page 30)

The Smugglers' Inn at Osmington Mills

Walks

On the following pages are some suggestions for short walks that can be enjoyed by all the family. All feature points of interest, either historical, natural or both. Use is made of six figure grid references and you are advised to use the relevant OS Explorer maps. There are also suggestions for where to eat and drink and advice about taking dogs.

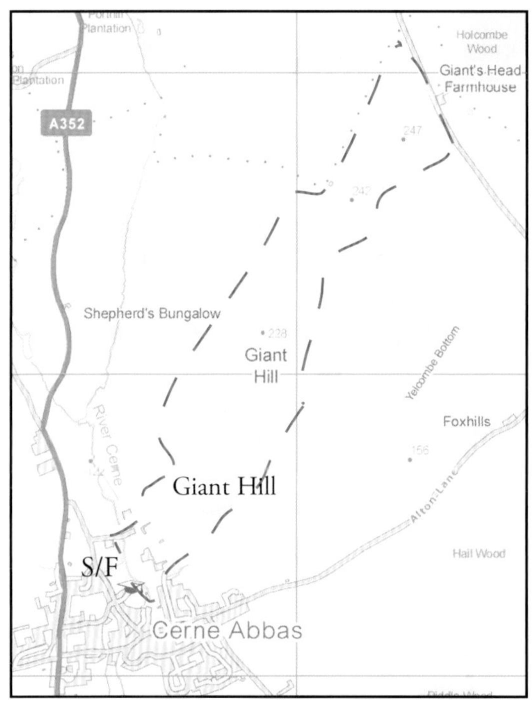

Notes: One reasonably steep climb, easy thereafter. Allow time to look at abbey.

Walk 1 - Cerne Abbas

(OS Explorer 117)

Length: 3.5 miles
Time: Allow 2 hours
Starting Point: ST 664015

The starting point for this walk is a car park and picnic area. From here continue up the small track towards Giant Hill, turn left by the barn and almost immediately right, still following signs to Giant Hill. At the foot of the hill, go through the gate into the woods and turn left up some steps. Follow the path round the bottom of the Giant (almost due north). Follow the contour of the hill for a while then, when faced with a choice of path, keep right and walk up the hill. When you reach a large open field go across the stile, turn left and follow the edge of the field. At the corner of a small wood the field boundary turns sharply left. Here there is a signposted path across the field. If you follow this at the other side of the field you will reach our return path to Cerne Abbas. Turn right.

Alternatively, continue round the edge of the field until you reach a road. Turn right and follow the road past the caravan park. Shortly after this on the right you will see a path on the right that follows the side of the large field.

Follow this path downhill, keeping left when faced with a choice. Near the bottom of the hill follow the signs to the village and abbey. Go through the churchyard and opposite the pond turn right up a small lane. Turn right over the stream and follow it back to the picnic area.
Eating and drinking – Plenty of pubs and cafes in Cerne Abbas, plus the walk starts in a pretty picnic area with tables.
Dogs - Good but note that they may have to be on the lead if animals are grazing.

Walk 2 - Osmington Mills and Ringstead Bay (OS map OL 15)

This walk can be done from either of two starting points. There is a large car park at Ringstead Bay with a shop and café or you may prefer to start from Osmington Mills. Here the car park belongs to the pub, The Smugglers' Inn, but you can often park in the road out of season.

From Osmington you will need to start by going round the back of the pub and joining the coast path to Ringstead Bay. This is easy to follow and at Ringstead follow the tarmac road past the car park. Continue on the road for a little while, round the bend to the left and just before a white house turn left on a path into woodland. Continue on the path through the woodland, following signs to Osmington Mills. You will go uphill past a thatched cottage and then follow a small road back into Osmington Mills.

By the holiday chalets you need to take a small path on the left by a fence. You will come out at a holiday park from where you can follow the road back down to the start point.
Eating and drinking: The Smugglers' Inn at Osmington or the café at Ringstead.
Dogs: No problem, they are allowed on the beach at both places.
Notes: Easy and straightforward, but you may want to begin at Ringstead.

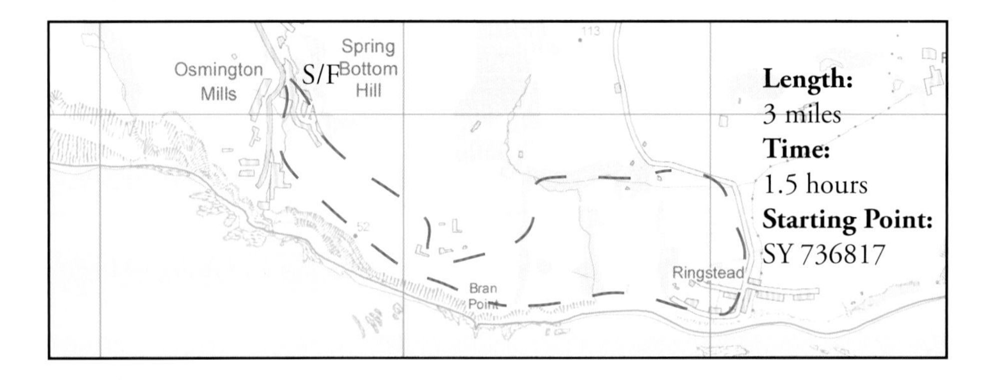

Above: The coast between Osmington Mills and Ringstead.

Walk 3 - Around Dorchester

There are a number of walks around Dorchester taking in different aspects of this historic town. The Tourist Information Centre in Antelope Walk has free maps and details. One suggestion is detailed below.

Start by the Dorset County Museum in High West Street, walk down the hill and turn left into North Square. Keep left up Friary Hill past Dorchester Prison. It was here that Thomas Hardy famously watched his first public hanging. Go past the prison and cross over the river on a small footbridge. Turn left along the river walk. Cross back over the river just before a thatched cottage. This is Hangman's Cottage, formerly the home of the prison's hangman. Carry on past the cottage and turn left down The Grove and past the statue of Thomas Hardy. Cross over High West Street into Albert Road and then keep left along West Walks and go through the gardens. At the end go right along Great Western Road and then left down Maumbury Road. Go left through the market and then right along Weymouth Avenue to Maumbury Rings and have a look around this well-preserved Roman amphitheatre. Retrace your steps down Weymouth Avenue but go across Great Western Road and then down South Street. You will emerge on High West Street near the museum.

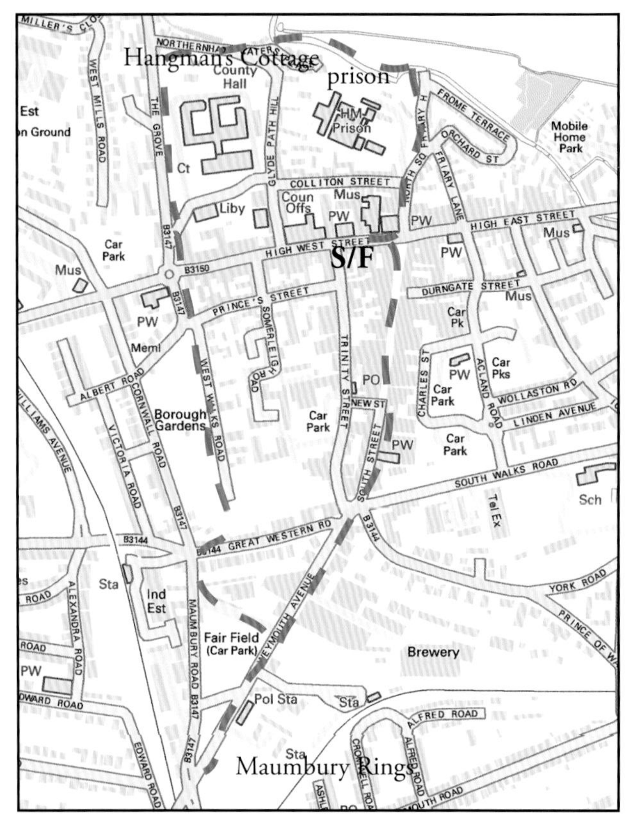

Length: 1-2 miles

Time: About 1 hour

Starting Point:
The county museum in High West Street.

Notes: Some busy roads to cross, but an easy walk.

Dogs: Not the best walk for dogs.

Eating and drinking:
Plenty of pubs, cafés and restaurants along the route.

Below: Hangman's Cottage, formerly the home of the official executioner at the prison.

Walk 4 - Langton Herring and the Fleet (OS map OL15)

In Langton Herring follow the road to the end of the village. There is a small layby near the sewage works. Take the path opposite the sewage works, turn left through the gate at the end and follow the path down to the Fleet. Then simply follow the coast path past Moonfleet Manor and to East Fleet where you can see the old church which was swamped in the tidal wave of 1824. Follow the little path past the church on to the road heading north-north west, past the new church. At the top of the road there is an entrance to a campsite; take the straight path to your right heading north. Turn left through another campsite [by the Red Barn] and follow the path back to the Fleet. Turn right following the sign to Langton Herring.

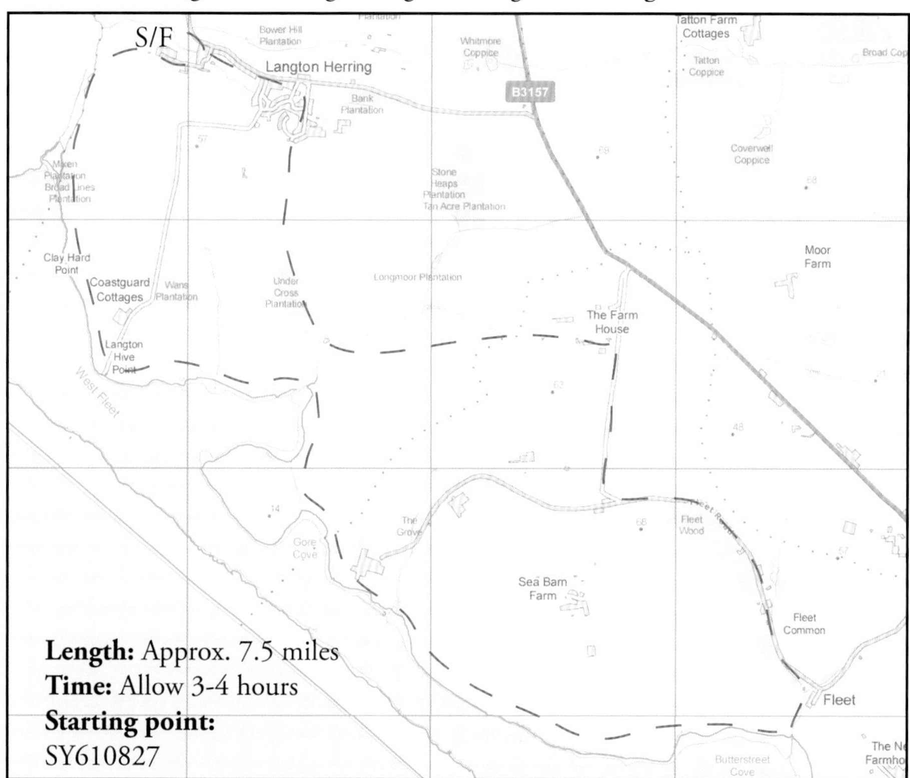

Length: Approx. 7.5 miles
Time: Allow 3-4 hours
Starting point:
SY610827

Notes: A fairly level walk with only one or two moderate climbs.
Eating and drinking:
The historic *Elm Tree Inn* at Langton Herring.
Dogs: Fine, but animals grazing in places and keep off racehorse gallops.

The Fleet at Rodden Hive (Langton Herring walk).

Walk 5 - Portland Bill (OS map OL15)

From the car park at Cheyne Weare follow the coast path south towards Portland Bill. You will have to follow the road for a short while before branching off on a track to the left marked "coast path". Follow this all the way to Portland Bill, past a number of old quarry sites on the cliffs.

After exploring Portland Bill go round the lighthouse and follow the coast path to the west. Go across the grassy area next to the MoD buildings and then take the path that follows the coast. At a stone marker just before the large buildings take the path to the right signed "East Cliff". Follow this path, keeping left when it appears to split [follow footpath signs]. You will reach a road where you should bear right and then, after a little while, bear right again . At the "Eight Kings" pub turn left at the mini-roundabout and follow the road back to the starting point.

Opposite: There are many old quarry workings on the east coast of Portland. Notice how the limestone slopes gently down towards the sea, ideal for loading into barges. In the centre is an old "whim" or crane.

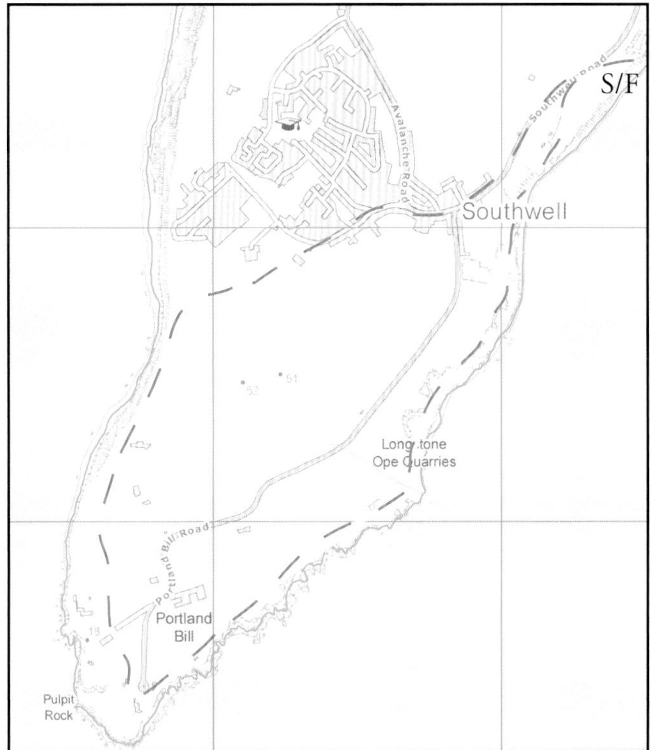

Length: 4 miles
Time: Allow 2.5 hrs.
Starting point: SY693704
Notes: An easy, level walk. You may want to allow time to wander around Portland Bill and see the visitor centre.
Eating and drinking: Café at Portland Bill - sit outside and admire the views.
Dogs: Fine with no restrictions but beware cliff edges.

Walk 6 - Abbotsbury (OS map OL15)

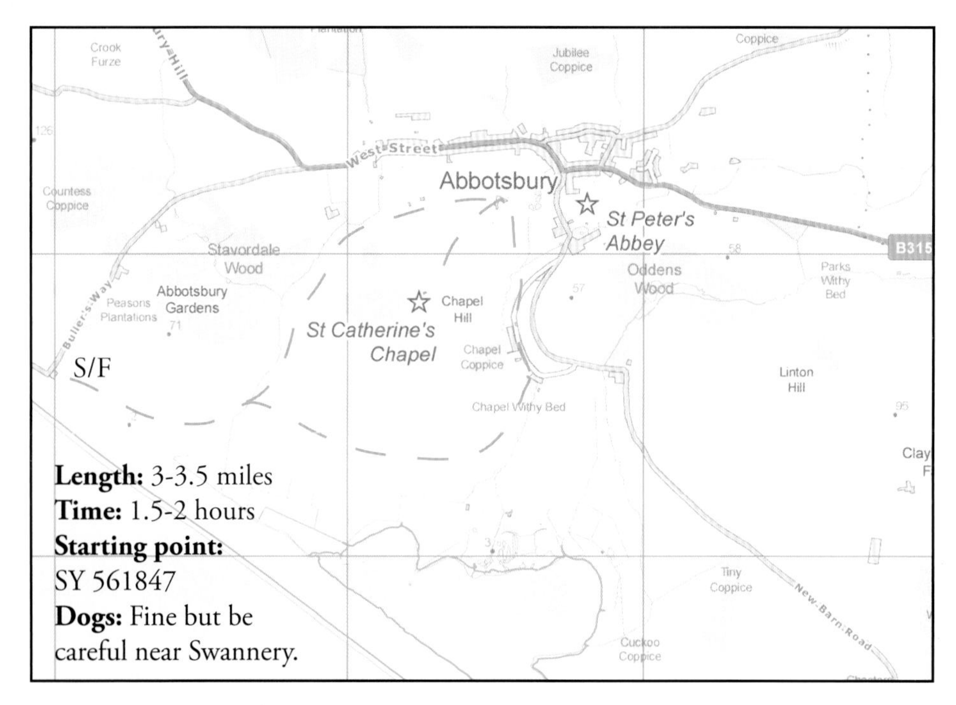

Length: 3-3.5 miles
Time: 1.5-2 hours
Starting point:
SY 561847
Dogs: Fine but be careful near Swannery.

From the car park follow the coast path alongside the beach towards Portland [at the bottom of the car park]. The path goes inland towards Abbotsbury. A little way along this stretch take the permissive path on the right to Abbotsbury Swannery (this is before the footpath marked on the OS map).When you reach a stile on your right go over this towards the Swannery and then left up the small road. Go up the road a little way then take a path on the left over a stile signed "Coast Path" and "Rope Walk". There is a wonderful, huge plane tree here.

Follow the path along the bottom of the hill but be sure to take a detour up the hill to St. Catherine's Chapel. This was quite possibly a sacred place well before Christianity came to these isles (see page 21). There are splendid views over Chesil Beach, the Fleet and the village of Abbotsbury.

Go back down the hill, turn left and follow the path back to Chesil Beach and the starting point.

Notes: A very easy walk; it is well worth the climb up the hill to St. Catherine's Chapel.

Eating and drinking: Plenty of pubs, cafés and restaurants in Abbotsbury.

Beach Guide

Weymouth – This is a perfect family beach with plenty of fine, golden sand and shallow, safe water. The sand here is renowned for the ease with which it is sculpted and there is a resident sand sculptor in the summer. Further east along the bay the beach is more shingle than sand. There are good car parks a little way behind the front. Naturally there are plenty of places to eat and drink and amusements. Weymouth may not be the place if you are looking for peace and quiet, but there is plenty to keep children occupied. Dogs are not allowed on the beach from the beginning of May until the end of September.

Bowleaze Cove – Situated at the eastern end of Weymouth Bay, just off the A353 as it turns away from the sea towards Preston. This is a safe, pebbly beach and dogs are allowed. There is a large holiday park at the cove and plenty of facilities, shops, café, pub and toilets. Being near a holiday park it is another lively, family beach. Plenty of car parking.

Osmington Mills – A small, rocky, pebbly beach at the end of a narrow road off the A353. This is a good place for scrambling over the rocks or for sitting quietly. Swimming is safe but the rocky shore means it is not ideal for children. The charming Smugglers' Inn is very popular and there is plenty of outdoor seating for when the sun is out. There is limited parking along the road and the small car park at the end of the road is for visitors to the inn. Dogs are allowed.

Looking east along Weymouth beach. Bowleaze Cove is at the far right.

Chesil Beach from the Isle of Portland.

Ringstead Bay – Just along the coast from Osmington, Ringstead is also reached via a narrow road from the A353. There is a long shingle beach although there is some sand exposed at low tide. It is safe to swim and dogs are allowed. There is a pay car park right next to the beach with a café, shop and toilets. There is a free car park at the top of the cliffs but it is a long walk to the beach! There are lovely views of Weymouth Bay from the beach.

Church Ope Cove – Beaches are few and far between on Portland but Church Ope Cove is a charming, quiet spot with safe swimmimg. It is situated just past the village of Easton on the east side of the isle. There is a small, free car park on the opposite side of the road and the track down to the beach goes past the interesting Portland Museum. It is a fairly steep walk down steps to the pebbly beach. Although swimming is safe, beware of going outside the cove, currents are notoriously strong off Portland. Dogs are allowed and there are toilets at the beach.

Chesil Beach – The beach can be accessed from a number of places. One of the easiest is the pay car park at the end of the road past the Sub-tropical Gardens in Abbotsbury. You will always find fishermen with their lines cast out to sea. It can be strangely relaxing to sit on top of the ridge of shingle and listen to the sea surging in and out, dragging the pebbles with it. Not the place to swim however, the water deepens very quickly and there are often strong currents. Dogs are allowed and there are toilets at the access points at Abbotsbury, Ferrybridge and West Weares on Portland.

Useful websites and telephone numbers:

Weymouth TIC - 01305 785747
www.weymouth.gov.uk
www.visitweymouth.co.uk
Dorchester TIC - 01305 267992
www.westdorset.com
www.visit-dorchester.co.uk
www.abbotsbury-tourism.co.uk
www.cerneabbas.org.uk
www.dorsetforyou.com
www.jurassiccoast.com

Public transport:

Both Weymouth and Dorchester are accessible by rail. Local bus services are provided by Wilts and Dorset and First.
www.wdbus.co.uk (01983 827005)
www.firstgroup.com
The "dorsetforyou" website has much information as do TICs.

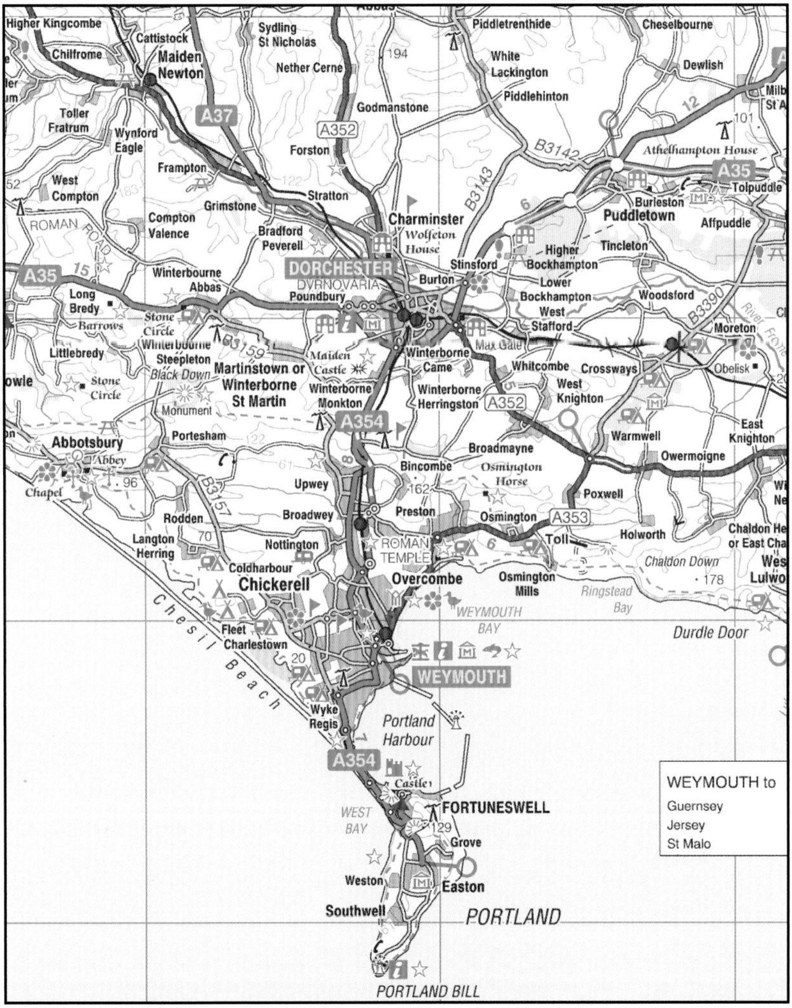

Other titles by ***Inspiring Places Publishing:***

Fossils and Rocks of the Jurassic Coast
The Jurassic Coast Illustrated
Smugglers' Dorset
Historic Dorset
Mysterious Places of Dorset
Dark Age Dorset
The Life and Works of Thomas Hardy
A brief guide to Purbeck
Day Tours in the East of Dorset
Mystery Big Cats of Dorset
Ancient Dorset

All titles are widely available around Dorset or can be ordered online at:

www.inspiringplaces.co.uk

The author:

Robert Westwood is a Dorset based writer and photographer. He studied geology at Exeter University and has written walking guides on the Jurassic Coast for the Jurassic Coast Trust. He also organises guided and self-guided walking breaks on the Isle of Purbeck.
There is more information at: *www.jurassiccoastwalking.co.uk*

Front cover: The old harbour at Weymouth with, inset, Chesil Beach from Portland.
Rear cover: Borough Gardens, Dorchester